IMAGES
of America

PETERSBURG

JOHN AND INA TYNES. The couple lived at 305 South Jefferson Street and had this portrait made January 5, 1947. Mr. Tynes was assistant secretary-treasurer of the Roper Company, a wholesale grocer.

IMAGES
of America

PETERSBURG

Suzanne K. Durham

ARCADIA
PUBLISHING

Published by Arcadia Publishing
Charleston, South Carolina

Library of Congress Catalog Card Number: 2003110504

For all general information contact Arcadia Publishing at:
Telephone 843-853-2070
Fax 843-853-0044
E-mail sales@arcadiapublishing.com
For customer service and orders:
Toll-Free 1-888-313-2665

Visit us on the Internet at www.arcadiapublishing.com

Dedicated to Herbert "Sonny" Rudlin

WILLIAM E. LUM JR. The photographer is photographed with his children, from left to right, Natalie, Howard, Wilma, and Ben, probably in the early 1930s. (Courtesy of the Lum family.)

CONTENTS

ACKNOWLEDGMENTS

My unreserved gratitude goes to Laura Willoughby, Curator Extraordinaire, and Karen Dale, Photo Coordinator to the Stars. Both ladies deserve to be treated like royalty for their dedication to making this book a quality product. Background support was gratefully received from Suzanne Savery and George Bass. Photos used in this book would not have been available without financial support and permission from the City of Petersburg. Mr. Lum's descendants—son Howard and daughter-in-law Jean—were most gracious in providing their personal touches to a book about an era long gone. I am just sorry that Mr. Lum's daughter, Wilma, was not able to share in this work. Cheerful research assistance was provided by Ann Brown, Florence Atkins, William Rinker, Evelyn Franklin, Gene Ross, Betty Eley, Lucious Edwards, and Chris Calkins. Extra special thanks go to H. Howard Hudgins Jr. for stepping into the breach.

INTRODUCTION

William Eldridge Lum Jr. was going to follow in his father's footsteps and become a druggist in the Lum Brothers pharmacy. His true talent—photography—emerged early, however, and he became the unofficial chronicler of the lives and events of Petersburg, Virginia, for nearly 30 years, from the 1920s through the Depression and World War II.

It is estimated there are more than 20,000 negatives surviving from his career, all of which have been donated to the Petersburg City Museums by Lum's family. This book is just a glimpse into the treasures of history contained in the Lum Collection. While most negatives were identified by date and carried some kind of description, it is hoped that readers will be able to fill in the identities of many of the people and places in these pictures from their own memories.

Lum was born June 12, 1889, in Ettrick, Virginia, across the Appomattox River from Petersburg. His father, William E. Lum, and uncle, Charles Lum, operated a drugstore in Ettrick. Around the turn of the century, the Lum brothers moved the store to 107 West Washington Street in Petersburg. After attending school, including a time at Fork Union Military Academy, Lum Jr. apprenticed in his father's pharmacy to become a druggist. Though he became qualified to be a druggist, he pursued photography instead and the rest—as they say—is Petersburg's history.

After working as the "Kodak department manager" in his father's drugstore, Lum opened his own photo studio in 1926 at 15 North Sycamore Street. After his death, the store was operated by one of his daughters. Only during the 1990s did the store become a branch of a Richmond camera shop. However, the storefront still carries the Lum sign.

Lum—called William E., Bill, or even Billy—dominated the photography business in Petersburg and surrounding communities such as Hopewell, Colonial Heights, and Ettrick. A large man and chain smoker, he was a familiar figure on the sidelines of the Petersburg High School football games with his camera on a tripod. He provided pictures of the high school football games for the Richmond newspapers and did many photo assignments for the Petersburg *Progress-Index*. He photographed car wrecks and building disasters for insurance companies and events for area schools, including Virginia State College (now a university). Lum was invited into people's homes to capture birthday parties, family portraits, Christmas trees, and the catch from fishing trips. He photographed corpses at funeral home viewings and soldiers at Camp Lee. His wedding photography could fill an entire book. It is also significant that Lum's collection features Petersburg's African-American citizens during a time when segregation and Jim Crow ruled.

A significant portion of his work focused on the retail and commercial trade. Lum was active in the Retail Merchants Association and served as state president at one time. Every year the city celebrated "Boost Petersburg Week" when storefronts would feature special displays of goods manufactured and sold in Petersburg. Lum would photograph these storefronts, often at night to get better lighting on the display.

In his personal life, Lum was an active member of First Baptist Church, a Mason, and a member of the Lions Club. Politically, he was a Democrat, but he never talked about his politics, according to his family. Lum and his wife, Eunice, had four children: Natalie, a pediatrician in Petersburg, and Ben, a financial planner, both now deceased; Wilma, who worked in the Lum store all her life; and Howard, a chemist who retired in Petersburg after living in New York and California most of his life. Lum himself died of cancer on February 5, 1951, and is buried in Blandford Cemetery.

History in Petersburg has traditionally meant the Civil War. Yet in these pages a new Petersburg history is recorded, thanks to the photographic career of William E. Lum Jr.

WILLIAM E. LUM JR. Lum was a very young man when photographed by the LaFrance Studio in Petersburg. (Courtesy of the Lum family.)

One

BUSINESS AND INDUSTRY

In the early 20th century, Petersburg supported a wide array of industries, including agricultural products from tobacco, cotton, peanuts, and lumber. It had two granite quarries and a shipyard at its Appomattox River port. At one time, it supported 11 trunk and valise factories and was considered the country's leading manufacturer of that product.

GEORGE BRASFIELD & COMPANY, MAY 29, 1946. These workers are filling boxes with thermostats for the electric blankets made at the factory at 310 Canal Street.

MAKING SUITCASES. In this undated photo, one of Petersburg's several valise factories creates the shaped wood frames around which fabric or leather would be applied to create a suitcase.

AMERICAN HARDWARE COMPANY BANQUET, JANUARY 1937. The luggage business began in 1870 with Simon Seward. In the 20th century, several Petersburg factories were consolidated under the name American Hardware.

PEANUT SHELLER, MAY 1933. This machine was housed at the Appomattox Ironworks located at 24 West Old Street. Peanuts were the city's fourth-largest export in the early 20th century.

ANDREW JOYNER COMPANY, JANUARY 14, 1938. The ironworks company was located at 30 South Union Street.

AMERICAN TELEPHONE COMPANY BANQUET, OCTOBER 25, 1940. Business was definitely a man's world as this company dinner shows.

PETERSBURG GAS COMPANY, JUNE 1930. Located at the corner of East Bank and Madison Streets, the plant featured a pyrometer.

JONES HATCHERY, DECEMBER 16, 1947. This youngster's mother hovers as he delights in being perched among the fuzzy chicks. Owned by Robert L. Jones, the chicken farm was located at 236 Hamilton Avenue in Colonial Heights.

A.G. Burcham, October 23, 1948. The motorcycle repair shop at 1460 West Washington Street was run by the same family that owns Burcham's Cycles today in Colonial Heights.

Petersburg Artificial Limb Company, May 5, 1947. The Hopkins Bros. storefront displays products of the prosthetics maker at 124 West Tabb Street.

DELTA OIL COMPANY, SEPTEMBER 12, 1946. "Call Dr. Delta" was the slogan for the company's burner service.

WRECKED CAR THAT KILLED MR. HENRY, MARCH 30, 1934. This totaled automobile was stored in the garage of the Standard Oil Company, which had several Petersburg locations. Lum routinely photographed wrecked cars and accident scenes for insurance companies.

GEORGE BRASFIELD LOADING A BOXCAR, JUNE 12, 1946. The Petersburg electric blanket factory used the railroad to transport its goods. Petersburg was at the junction of three national rail lines.

The sign on the testing tank reads:

90000 LB. LOAD
TEST ON ONE
RAYMOND CONCRETE PILE

TESTING TANK, AUGUST 4, 1950. The Raymond Concrete Pile Company tested its product in the early phases of construction of the Petersburg hospital on South Adams Street.

"FIVE AND TEN" KRESGE STORE, FEBRUARY 20, 1942. The store at 112–114 North Sycamore Street underwent an expansion during World War II. Archie Collins was store manager.

A.H. SNYDER PRINTING. This Ettrick business had several locations including Chesterfield Avenue and Light Avenue.

PRODUCTS OF AMERICAN HARDWARE COMPANY, MAY 5, 1947. In a citywide promotion, storefronts featured special displays of goods manufactured in Petersburg. This display was featured at Lavenstein's on North Sycamore Street.

PHOTO-FINISHING DEPARTMENT, APRIL 28, 1947. The Lum photo store processed film, provided studio photography, and sold stationery and office supplies.

PETERSBURG MOTOR COMPANY, 1950. The city's Ford dealership, 10 North Market Street, also featured a body shop (above). Below, the sales and service employees line up for a photo.

CARNIVAL TRACTOR TRAILER, MARCH 27, 1946. Industry and history are the city's selling points in an optimistic display of boosterism at the Petersburg city fair.

Two

MERCHANTS

"Boost Petersburg Week" was an annual business celebration marked by special displays in the storefronts downtown. Before malls existed, Petersburg downtown was a thriving shopping center featuring stores that sold everything from furniture to groceries to clothing.

SOUTHWORTH'S DRUGSTORE, MAY 29, 1947. This display was put up for National Baby Week at the corner drugstore on North Sycamore and Washington Streets.

BEER DISPLAY, JANUARY 17, 1940. The Elite Cigar Store at 133 North Sycamore Street also

featured a pool hall. The owner was John R. Jennings.

CHARLES LEONARD HARDWARE COMPANY, MAY 11, 1946. This truckload of agriculture sprayers was delivered to the hardware store at 20–24 West Bank Street.

NURSE'S WINDOW DISPLAY, JANUARY 16, 1947. Promoting nursing classes, this display in the Rucker Rosenstock store featured a portrait of local nurse Margaret Falls. The store was located at 132 North Sycamore Street.

Hams, March 14, 1947. The Big Star Store at 401 Bank Street priced its ham in a way to catch the shopper's eye—$980 per ton.

MARY LEE ICE CREAM COMPANY, DECEMBER 1, 1936. The confectioner's store had locations at 143 Halifax Street and 247 North Sycamore Street.

COCA-COLA BOTTLING WORKS, MAY 5, 1947. The display for Boost Petersburg Week was set up in the storefront of the Morris & Claytor men's furnishings shop at 103 North Sycamore Street.

GULF OIL STATION, AUGUST 19, 1941. This service station, with an attendant waiting to fill your tank, was located at 723 West Washington Street.

MORRIS PLAN BANK, 1930. Chief of traffic police, Charles E. King, keeps an eye on the crowds in front of the bank at 121 North Sycamore Street. Notice the clock says it is 9 p.m.

ATKINS BATTERY & VULCANIZING, NOVEMBER 1929. Auto tires and batteries were sold at this store located at 119 West Bank Street.

CAROLE KING WINDOW, SEPTEMBER 25, 1940. "Fall fashions of the hour" are displayed in a storefront of A.L. Lavenstein's, located at 109–111 North Sycamore Street.

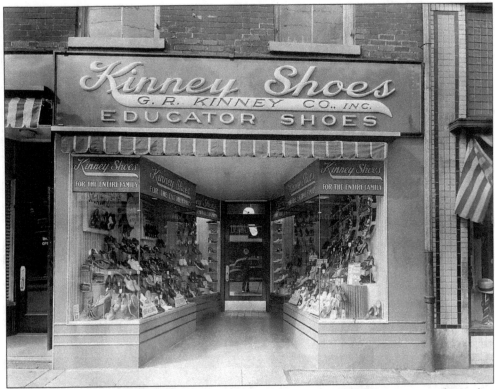

KINNEY SHOES, MARCH 6, 1939. The familiar chain store for family footwear was located at 10 North Sycamore Street.

LOCK DISPLAY, JUNE 22, 1951. This photo was taken at Charles Leonard Hardware on West Bank Street.

Minton Meat Market, 1936. John W. Minton owned this market at the corner of Hinton and West Streets. It looks like eggs were 25¢ a dozen.

FRANKLIN FURNITURE, APRIL 4, 1950. The furniture store was located on the northwest corner of Sycamore and Bank Streets, where Longstreet's Restaurant is now. After tornado damage in the early 1990s, the furniture store closed.

NEW MARKET RESTAURANT, APRIL 7, 1949. Owned by Jerry Litos, Peter Valanidas, and Peter Kapsidelis, New Market Restaurant was located at 127 Halifax Street. It segregated its patrons with counters that faced each other.

COLONIAL STORE, JUNE 17, 1949. Tender green beans threatened to spill over at the grocery store at 40 East Bank Street. According to the sign, the beans were sold for about 8¢ a pound.

MECCA RESTAURANT, C. 1941. Gus and Mabel Kappas operated this eatery at 1411 West Washington Street. They lived above the restaurant for a time, later moving to 1415 West Washington Street.

MECCA RESTAURANT, INTERIOR, C. 1941. Notice the stove in the middle of the restaurant. This stretch of West Washington Street is vacant today.

J.W. Rackley Company. This undated photo shows one of a number of grocers and meat markets in an area of Petersburg along South Avenue and Halifax Street called City Market.

Three

MILITARY LIFE

Fort Lee—originally Camp Lee—came into existence to process soldiers during World War I. It closed until World War II brought it back into operation. Segregated facilities were standard during the time of these photos.

PLAYING ORGAN, NOVEMBER 14, 1950. A young soldier is practicing his music at Camp Lee.

AMERICAN LEGION DEDICATION, MAY 30, 1943. This Memorial Day ceremony was held on the lawn of City Hall to commemorate the soldiers killed in World War II. The permanent memorial marker was dedicated in 1948.

WYTHE STREET USO, OCTOBER 18, 1948. These two Women's Army Corp (WAC) recruits are sewing at the service club at 303 Wythe Street.

BYRNE STREET USO, OCTOBER 18, 1948. Two African-American soldiers arrive at the USO club at 460 Byrne Street.

NAVY MOTHERS, JANUARY 16, 1947. These women are new officers in the Navy Mothers club at the YMCA.

MANAGERS AND OPERATORS, DECEMBER 24, 1946. This is the C&P Telephone center at Camp Lee. These servicemen are probably making holiday calls home to their families.

SNACK BAR, JUNE 13, 1951. The USO club on Byrne Street offered food and friendship to African-American servicemen.

CAMP LEE DANCE, NOVEMBER 15, 1946. In this photo, the 26th Company holds a dance at Camp Lee. According to the custom of the times, social affairs were segregated.

VIRGINIA NATIONAL GUARD, 1936. This is the Medical Unit led by Petersburg physician Dr. James E. Smith (front row, fourth from right).

PETERSBURG AIRPORT, DECEMBER 8, 1943. The airport in Dinwiddie County was established by the Civil Aviation Authority to provide coastal Army planes with additional landing fields. After the war, the city bought the airfield. The civilian in this photo is R.L. Arnold, owner of the ink pen manufacturer in Petersburg.

THE CRATER. The site of Petersburg's most spectacular Civil War battle is heavily commemorated. Confederate war veteran Carter R. Bishop (above, to the left of the monument) was a founding member of the Petersburg Battlefield Park Association, which was founded in 1926. This is probably the date of the photo. Below, re-enactors line up along the edge of the crater in a dedication and pageant ceremony for the Petersburg National Military Park on June 20, 1932.

BANQUET, MARCH 7, 1946. Sergeant Quinn's 18th Battalion, 98th Quartermaster Training Company held a party at Alford's Restaurant, located at the corner of South Sycamore and Winfield Streets.

PETERSBURG NATIONAL MILITARY PARK, MAY 21, 1950. These tourists are in the Crater, a practice that was stopped in the 1970s. The monument in the background was dedicated in 1924 to honor South Carolina's Elliott Brigade.

War Veterans, October 30, 1946. These young men attended Petersburg High School before serving in the military. This photo was taken for the school yearbook, *The Missile*.

VFW, 1947. New officers are sworn in at the Veterans of Foreign Wars meeting.

NAVY FOOTBALL TEAM, 1944. Ben Lum, left, son of the photographer, and Dan Williams played football while serving in the military. They later married sisters, Jean and Ellen Bakelaar.

Four

EDUCATION

Virginia State University—formerly a college—offered African Americans an education equivalent to other state schools including clubs, Greek life, and prominent visitors such as Nobel Peace prize winner Ralph Bunche and singer Marian Anderson. Lum did much of the photography for the college yearbook, The Trojan. Likewise, Petersburg High School was a frequent subject of Lum's photography; many of his pictures were used in the school yearbook, The Missile.

GIRLS HOCKEY TEAM, 1937. The team lines up for a photo outside Petersburg High School.

GLEE CLUB, NOVEMBER 15, 1937. Lum took many photos for Virginia State College (now a university), including its yearbook, *The Trojan.*

NURSES HOME, 1938. The Petersburg Hospital taught students at 7 North Madison Street.

GRADUATION PARADE, JUNE 2, 1940. Pictured above is the processional at the Virginia State College commencement.

PETERSBURG HIGH SCHOOL GRADUATION, JUNE 7, 1940. Petersburg High School students were graduated in ceremonies at Cameron Field.

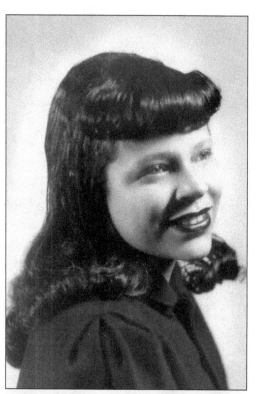

MARY GWENDOLYN COLES, APRIL 6, 1948. Miss Coles sits for her senior portrait. She graduated from Virginia State College in 1948 with a degree in Home Economics.

ORCHESTRA, DECEMBER 6, 1940. The Virginia State College orchestra poses for a yearbook photo.

NEW FARMERS, AUGUST 5, 1944. The national convention of the New Farmers of America was held at Virginia State College.

NON-ATHLETIC GIRLS CLUB, 1945. This club showed its school spirit without participating in sports. They are seated on the steps of Petersburg High School.

TROMBONE SECTION, OCTOBER 30, 1946. This Petersburg High School band photo was taken on Cameron Field for the yearbook, *The Missile*.

RANDY MALLORY, 1945. This Petersburg High School football player poses at Cameron Field. A year earlier, the school was state football champion.

GRADUATE STUDENTS, MAY 4, 1945. These graduate students pose in front of Virginia Hall at Virginia State College.

OMEGA PSI PHI, MAY 15, 1945. These fraternity brothers gather at Virginia State College, probably an alumni reunion.

HOME ECONOMICS DISPLAY, OCTOBER 22, 1945. The home economics students at Virginia State College pose with handmade items for the Out-of-School Youth Conference.

MISS VIRGINIA STATE, OCTOBER 22, 1945. Contestants sit on the monument wall in front of Virginia Hall.

GIRLS' BASKETBALL TEAM, FEBRUARY 23, 1946. Petersburg High School's girls' basketball team poses in the gym.

BLANDFORD SCHOOL, APRIL 5, 1946. The elementary school for African-American children was located at 816 East Bank Street.

TRADE SCHOOL, MAY 9, 1946. Mechanical engineering or training was offered at Virginia State College.

COACH DAY, 1933. Roland C. Day, in the car, coached football at Petersburg High School. He is chatting with Carter Myers Jr., whose family owned Petersburg Motor Company.

WILMA LUM, MARCH 16, 1947. The photographer's daughter Wilma studied at Westhampton College (now the University of Richmond) and attended a college dance.

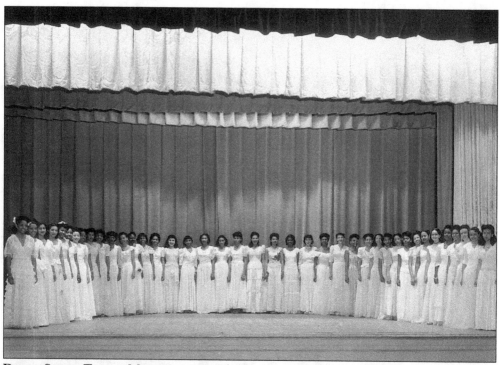

DELTA SIGMA THETA, MAY 14, 1946. The sorority appears on the Langston Hall stage at Virginia State College.

NURSES GRADUATION, MAY 17, 1946. Nursing students are honored at the Petersburg Country Club for completing their studies with the hospital.

SCHOOL CLASSROOM, MAY 30, 1946. The Blandford School was the grammar school for the African-American children of Petersburg.

ALUMNI, JUNE 1, 1946. These ladies are former graduates of Virginia State College.

PETERSBURG HIGH SCHOOL BAND, OCTOBER 30, 1946. The Petersburg High School band spells out "P" at the 50-yard line of Cameron Field.

ETTRICK PTA, FEBRUARY 4, 1947. These ladies are honored as past and current presidents of the Ettrick Parent-Teacher Association.

CHARLES O. CHRISTIAN, JANUARY 28, 1947. This 1949 graduate of Virginia State College went on to coach basketball at Norfolk State University.

JOURNALISM CLASS, FEBRUARY 11, 1947. These students are meeting in the public relations office of Virginia State College.

HONOR GRADUATES, MARCH 18, 1947. These young women earned academic honors at Virginia State College.

MISS HOMECOMING, OCTOBER 23, 1947. Virginia State College's candidates for the autumn celebration strike a casual pose.

LAVERNE YOUNG, OCTOBER 17, 1950. This student actress graduated from Virginia State College in 1952 and later taught music in Rockville, Maryland.

MODERN DANCE TROUPE, MAY 11, 1946. Performers make a dramatic picture on stage at Virginia State College.

COMMENCEMENT, MAY 29, 1950. Dr. Robert P. Daniel (left), president of Virginia State College, awards a degree to a student.

WRESTLERS AND BOXERS, FEBRUARY 24, 1950. Thomas Verdell (in a tuxedo) coached wrestling and boxing at Virginia State College.

FOOTBALL TEAM, SEPTEMBER 15, 1950. The Petersburg High School football team was state champion in 1933, 1937, 1944, and 1967. These players are posing on Cameron Field.

Five

CHURCHES AND
CHARITIES

Petersburg supported churches of all denominations. The state mental hospital for African Americans and the state colony for the mentally retarded, which became the Southside Training Center, were both located in Petersburg.

SUNDAY SCHOOL CONVENTION, 1939. Baptists met at Petersburg's First Baptist Church. Rev. William M. Thompson was the pastor at that time.

BRIGHT HOPE BIBLE CLASS, MAY 15, 1939. Church members pose in front of the Memorial M.E. Church at 1120 West Washington Street.

GROUND-BREAKING, JULY 15, 1940. Members of the Second Baptist Church hold a ground-breaking ceremony for an annex to the church when it was at 100 South Sycamore Street. The church is now located on Johnson Road.

ST. JAMES CATHOLIC CHURCH, JUNE 9, 1946. Pictured here are graduates of the Hopewell church's school.

CHENAULT BIBLE CLASS, OCTOBER 5, 1946. The men of Calvary Baptist Church, at the corner of High and South Streets, gather on the steps of the church.

BOARD OF STEWARDS, OCTOBER 7, 1946. The board of the Washington Street Methodist Church, on East Washington Street near Sycamore Street, sits for a picture.

COLORED BAPTIST ORPHANAGE, NOVEMBER 23, 1949. This home was the precursor to what is now the Children's Home of Virginia Baptists in Matoaca across from Shallow Baptist Church.

WOMEN'S MISSIONARY UNION GRADUATES, OCTOBER 1, 1950. The Women's Missionary Union (WMU) at First Baptist Church sponsored a children's program with categories of Royal Ambassadors (R.A.), Young Women's Association (Y.W.A.), Girls' Auxiliary (G.A.), and the Sunbeams.

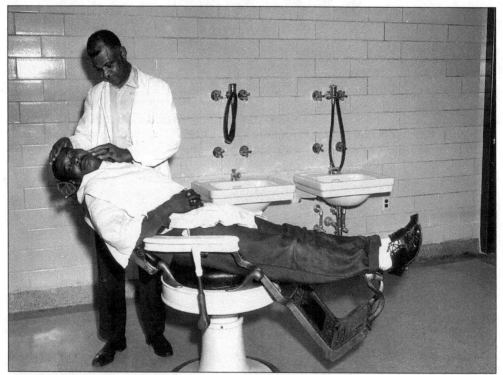

CENTRAL STATE HOSPITAL, JULY 12, 1952. The facility on Cox Road was originally intended for African-American "mental cases." This could be a photo of a patient getting ready for a shave or shampoo.

CHILDREN'S CHOIR. Though undated and unidentified, this photo depicts the innocence of children in churches everywhere. Notice the musical motif of the curtains.

WEST END BAPTIST CHURCH, DECEMBER 21, 1946. The choir at West End Baptist Church, 1017 West Washington Street, poses for a Christmas photo.

BABY CHRISTENING, OCTOBER 20, 1946. The Salvation Army, 124 West Bank Street, holds a group christening led by Capt. John R. Jones. If you look closely, you can see the photo was printed backwards; the signs on the wall are reversed.

PETERSBURG STATE COLONY. The facility, on Cox Road across from Central State Hospital, was later called the Petersburg Training School and is now the Southside Regional Training Center. It was originally intended for "feeble-minded" African American youth. Above, young people conduct May Day exercises on May 1, 1952. Below, a Christmas dinner awaits them on December 25, 1950.

CHURCH OF THE HOLY FAMILY, MAY 23, 1944. This Catholic church for African Americans was located at 237 Halifax Street. Previously, it was the Ebenezer Baptist Church. Fr. Joseph A. Stanton led the congregation.

Six

CLUBS AND ORGANIZATIONS

Benevolent, fraternal, social, and professional organizations were well represented in Petersburg. All types of citizens were involved—white, African-American, men, women, and children.

KIWANIS CLUB, NOVEMBER 20, 1934. The Petersburg Kiwanis pose at City Hall.

ELKS MEETING, FEBRUARY 5, 1941. The Elks hold a ceremonial meeting at their club located at 103 West Tabb Street.

LIONS CLUB, APRIL 1939. The Lions Club poses at City Hall, a popular setting for group pictures in Petersburg.

CHRISTMAS DINNER, DECEMBER 28, 1943. The Kiwanis Club sponsored a holiday outing for crippled children.

QUARTERBACK CLUB, AUGUST 28, 1946. The coaches of the city football league are posing at Globe Department store.

INDIAN SWAMP, MAY 17, 1946. This fishing club, still in existence, is located in Prince George County, near the Sussex County line. The photo was ordered by George B. Townsend,

an insurance agent who lived at 633 South Sycamore Street.

MOCK WEDDING, JANUARY 16, 1947. These boys at the YMCA are dressed up to simulate a wedding, even toting a shotgun to enforce the ceremony.

BUSINESS AND PROFESSIONAL WOMEN'S CLUB, APRIL 15, 1947. New officers are sworn in for the women's group.

KIWANIS CLUB PICNIC, JULY 16, 1947. The Kiwanis Club sponsored an outing to Dutch Gap for crippled children.

BLOOD-TYPING, JANUARY 22, 1948. The American Red Cross visited the C&P Telephone offices to obtain blood types. Area manager John Hesse, seated, is bravely getting stuck.

VOTING FROM CAR, APRIL 6, 1948. Mrs. Mary S. Moore, pictured at age 93, still voted with some assistance.

LIONS CLUB FLOAT. Given the patriotic theme of the sign on the float, this undated photo was probably taken during World War II.

EASTERN STAR OFFICERS, MARCH 12, 1948. The ladies' club poses at the Masonic Hall at 13 West Tabb Street.

4-H CLUB, JUNE 5, 1951. Virginia State College sponsored 4-H clubs for African American youth.

NAACP, March 22, 1950. The local chapter of the National Organization for the Advancement of Colored People meets at the Harding Street YMCA.

Knights of Pythias, July 24, 1952. The officers of the fraternal organization meet on the second floor of the Naomi Lodge located at 131–141 North Sycamore Street.

Seven

FAMILIES

Families wanted photographs of the important events in their lives, including birthday parties, family reunions, wedding anniversaries, and funerals.

MRS. DEFFENBAUGH AND FAMILY, JULY 20, 1946. Seated in the basement of Folly Castle, 323 West Washington Street, the Deffenbaugh family enjoys a meal. This was the location of a restaurant Mrs. Mary Deffenbaugh operated. Folly Castle was built by a descendant of Petersburg's founder, Peter Jones.

EMILY R. BURGWYN, 1929. Miss Burgwyn, a teacher at Duncan M. Brown grammar school on the corner of Wythe and Jefferson Streets, has her portrait made.

ANNIE MANN IN THE GARDEN, JUNE 1929. Miss Mann was the society editor of the Petersburg *Progress-Index*. Her home was located at 41 North Main Street, now Crater Road, in what was the Blandford section of town.

OFFICER DANIEL FAMILY. Ashton and Lottie Daniel had family portraits taken eight years apart. Above, in 1931, the family lived at 235 Lafayette Avenue in Colonial Heights. Below, looking quite aged, the policeman and his family are photographed at their home at 1104 Boulevard on June 29, 1939.

FRANK BUTLER FAMILY, NOVEMBER 9, 1936. Frank and Myrtle Butler lived at 234 Lee Avenue in Colonial Heights. Mr. Butler was the secretary-treasurer of the R.L. Arnold Pen Company.

FLORENCE ATKINS, C. 1945. This is a Lum studio portrait of Ms. Atkins, a bookkeeper for many years with the T.S. Beckwith Company, which sold office supplies.

BOLLING FAMILY REUNION, 1938. At least three generations are pictured here in the parlor of the Bolling home. The Bolling name is long associated with Centre Hill mansion, but it is not clear whether this family was directly related.

HARVEY SEWARD FAMILY, DECEMBER 5, 1938. Harvey Seward and his wife, Annie, owned the Ivy Gates mansion that stood in the 1000 block of South Sycamore Street, where an apartment complex is now. He was the president of the luggage manufacturer American Hardware Company.

MRS. E.H. TITMUS FUNERAL, MARCH 24, 1947. Mrs. Titmus was buried in her family plot in Blandford Cemetery. She was the wife of the president of Titmus Optical Company, which still operates today.

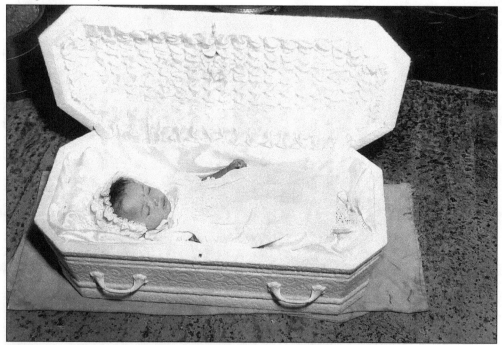

BABY IN A CASKET, DECEMBER 30, 1946. One of Lum's sad assignments was photographing the bodies of loved ones in their caskets. Here, a baby girl is photographed at the Jackson Funeral Home, 220 Halifax Street. Funeral establishments, along with other businesses, were segregated.

MR. AND MRS. ANDERSON, OCTOBER 23, 1946. This couple celebrates their 50th wedding anniversary.

MATTHEWS FAMILY, NOVEMBER 30, 1947. Albert and Carrie Matthews lived at 21 Liberty Street. He owned R.L. Matthews & Son wholesale grocers.

MISS ZIMMER AND MISS EDMOND, DECEMBER 12, 1947. Esther "Essie" Zimmer was the widow of W.L. Zimmer, president of the International Filler Corporation, which made bottle-filling machines. The dogs are not identified.

T.C. MORRIS FAMILY, DECEMBER 26, 1947. Looking like a *Father Knows Best* episode, this portrait features the family of Thomas and Elizabeth Morris, who lived at 1771 Westover Avenue. Thomas Morris worked for Solvay Processors, a chemical plant in Hopewell.

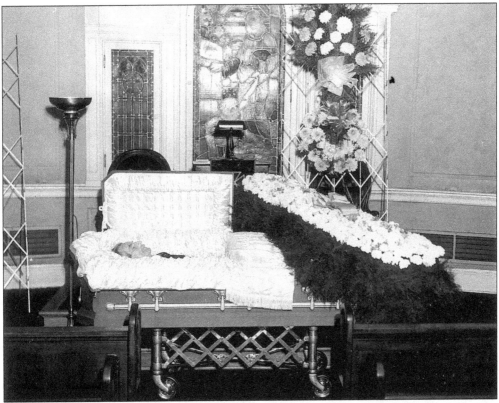

J.T. Morriss's Funeral Home, October 19, 1948. The Morriss's establishment has taken care of many generations of Petersburg's citizens. At the time of this photo, the funeral home was located at 1–3 South Sycamore Street.

Funeral Coach. This undated photo shows an early hearse owned by the J.T. Morriss's Funeral Home.

HAPPY BIRTHDAY! APRIL 5, 1947. What did the photographer tell these children to elicit these grins? This photo session was done for Mrs. J.D. Whitmore.

Eight

WEDDINGS

The entire nuptial traditions of couples in Petersburg and vicinity were photographed by Lum, from the bride's dressing room to the traditional rice-throwing. The candid shots are the most revealing.

DUNCAN-FORD WEDDING, JUNE 21, 1947. The happy couple dodges rice thrown in the time-honored tradition.

CAMP LEE WEDDING, JULY 7, 1948. Sgt. and Mrs. Jack T. Lillie were married at the military base.

COALEY-PHELPS WEDDING, AUGUST 21, 1948. This beautiful bride posed for a studio portrait.

GANDY WEDDING, AUGUST 1934. Bride Marian Gandy, daughter of Dr. John M. Gandy, who was president of Virginia State College, poses with her stylish wedding party.

BRIDAL PARTY, C. 1951. The bare trees and condensation from car exhaust indicate it is a winter wedding in this unidentified photo.

WILLIAMS WEDDING. "Look Ma, no hands" is some of the graffiti applied to the honeymoon car in this undated photo.

JUST MARRIED! This unidentified couple just got hitched at the historic Calvary Episcopal Church in Dinwiddie.

HELEN DAVIS WEDDING, 1935. The bride was a clerk at the Peoples Life Insurance Company, though after marriage, she probably stayed home, as was the custom.

POWELL-GLASS WEDDING, OCTOBER 11, 1948. The bride is assisted by her attendant before the ceremony. Lum composed his photos with care; notice the reflections in the mirror and the small portrait on the vanity.

POWELL-GLASS WEDDING, OCTOBER 11, 1948. The more spontaneous moments are also caught on film.

CHURCH WEDDING. In a traditional formal photo, the wedding party gathers at the front of the church. This undated photo shows many of the decorative traditions of the ceremony, such as ribbons on each row of pews.

MOTHER OF THE BRIDE. It is likely the bride's mother is adjusting the bride's veil while her mother-in-law or doting aunt straightens her skirt.

GOODI WEDDING, JUNE 14, 1952. This photo is half posed and half candid. The two women on the right are engaged in intense conversation while the bride patiently awaits instructions. Her father looks for the car that will take them to the church.

Nine

LEISURE

What did Petersburg do for fun? Fishing was a favorite, as were sports, music, and fashion shows.

MAGICIAN ON STAGE, MARCH 16, 1934. Allen R. Keyes is ready to make some magic. His day job was as a salesman at Petersburg Motor Company.

CARNIVAL, MARCH 27, 1946. Paradise Revue performers pose for the camera. The city held a fair annually, similar to a county fair with rides, game booths, and other midway attractions.

TUBIZE MAY QUEEN, APRIL 28, 1930. Evelyn Morris, dressed in a gown of artificial silk—or rayon—made by the Tubize Chatillon Corporation, is crowned queen in the May Day celebration. The factory was located at 1231 Commerce Street.

CHRISTMAS PARTY, DECEMBER 20, 1946. The C&P Telephone Company hosts a holiday dance at the Petersburg Country Club for its employees. The country club was located on Johnson Road.

FIRST BAPTIST CHURCH, JULY 17, 1946. Church-goers play softball on a summer evening. These games were played at Lee Park—without lights.

PETERSBURG MUSIC CLUB, FEBRUARY 18, 1947. Local president Mildred Squires (left) and state president Mrs. Franklin pose at the home of Mrs. Westmore Brown.

WILKERSON SUNRISE RAMBLERS, JANUARY 18, 1947. The bluegrass band plays at Grant's Dance Hall on Route 1 "a mile beyond Richie's store."

41 POUNDS OF FISH, FEBRUARY 8, 1947. From left to right, Paul Adams, G.E. Seay, and Randolph Blankenship pose in Lum's store with their catch of the day.

TRI-HI-G FASHION SHOW, MAY 21 1947. Joy Vaughn models a bathing suit on the stage at Petersburg High School. Note the live music provided by an orchestra.

CIRCUS. What would a circus be without a freak show? The annual fair was held at the fairgrounds on Farmer Street.

WSSV CHARACTER SKETCH, JUNE 2, 1948. Don Blake (standing) and Lou Ross cut up during what was an otherwise straight photo shoot. Blake was the announcer and Ross a disc jockey at the radio station located at 112 West Tabb Street.

More Fish, August 12, 1948. Gen. M.S. Carter (left) and Col. J.K. Waters pose with their catch. The officers might have been stationed at Camp Lee.

MR. LUM AND FISH. Here is an undated photo of the photographer with his fish. One wonders if he could have used a timer on his camera to create a self-portrait. The hat was one of his trademarks.

PARK DRIVE-IN. The drive-in theatre was located east of town at 2400 East Bank Street. Ford's 50th anniversary was in 1953. Another drive-in was located south of town on Crater Road.

SENATOR MAPP AND PARTY, MAY 21, 1929. Democratic state Sen. G. Walter Mapp (third from right) represented Accomack County from 1912 to 1923. He served as Commissioner of Fisheries during that time.

YMCA Boys at the Pool, June 16, 1946. Standards of modesty were different 50 years ago; small swimmers are in the buff. The YMCA was located at 128–130 North Union Street.